TURTLES

By Robert J. Church

Photos by the author

Distributed in the U.S.A. by T.F.H. Publications, Inc., 211 West Sylvania Avenue, P.O. Box 27, Neptune City, N.J. 07753; in England by T.F.H. (Gt. Britain) Ltd., 13 Nutley Lane, Reigate, Surrey; in Canada to the book store and library trade by Clarke, Irwin & Company, Clarwin House, 791 St. Clair Avenue West, Toronto 10, Ontario; in Canada to the pet trade by Rolf C. Hagen Ltd., 3225 Sartelon Street, Montreal 382, Quebec; in Southeast Asia by Y.W. Ong, 9 Lorong 36 Geylang, Singapore 14; in Australia and the south Pacific by Pet Imports Pty. Ltd., P.O. Box 149, Brookvale 2100, N.S.W., Australia. Published by T.F.H. Publications Inc. Ltd., The British Crown Colony of Hong Kong.

ISBN 0-87666-226-2

CONTENTS

Cover photograph courtesy of Armstrong Cork Company, manufacturer of the beautiful Tessera Corlon floor covering on which the boy and his turtle play.

The author holds a young baby African tortoise. Although turtles cannot respond with displays of affection the way some other pets can, they are fascinating pets nevertheless.

1. About Turtles in General

INTRODUCTION

Turtles have been turtles for 200 million years or so, which is about 199 million years longer than people have been people.

Turtles were here when the giant dinosaurs were lumbering around scaring the daylights out of everything, and they were here when the thunder of the giants died away. They were here when *Hyracotherium*, the dawn horse, foaled, and they were here when *we* finally stood up on our hind legs and started telling each other that the whole universe was built just for us.

Turtles have come plodding out of the mists of prehistory, virtually untouched by evolution. While everything around them was changing, they remained for the most part unchanged. Turtles are built to last.

Turtles have sacrificed mobility for the protection of a stout shell.

A turtle's shell is always functional, and often beautiful. It is an architectural triumph, usually made of bone with an outer covering of hornlike material similar in substance to our fingertails. The top shell is called the *carapace*,

Turtles breathe air and must make occasional trips to the surface to replenish their supply of oxygen.

the bottom one the *plastron*, and connecting the two on each side are the *bridges*. A turtle's shell is an integral part of its body; the animal cannot live without it.

EATING AND ELIMINATION

Instead of teeth, a turtle has a horny beak and a hard crushing surface in the roof of its mouth. It utilizes these structures to reduce food to small pieces before swallowing.

A turtle's digestive tract and excretory system both empty into a common organ, the cloaca, from which body waste is eliminated. A similar situation occurs in birds and sharks.

BREATHING

All turtles have lungs and breathe air. They can stay under water for prolonged periods, but they must eventually come to the surface. If they don't, they'll drown.

BODY TEMPERATURE

Although mammals and birds have an automatic temperature control system that maintains the body temperature at a constant level, a turtle's body temperature varies with that of his surroundings. To avoid dangerously low or high body temperatures, certain turtles may hibernate in the winter or estivate in the summer. In either case, the turtle seeks out a sheltered site and passes through the critical period in a dormant state.

Captive turtles usually cannot hibernate or estivate at will, but must rely on their owners to maintain a livable temperature for them. Temperature control is of great importance in the successful maintenance of captive turtles.

REPRODUCTION

Male turtles possess an intromittent organ, within the cloaca, about midway between the base and tip of the tail. This organ can be protruded from the body to transport sperm from the male's cloaca to the female's; it does not serve a urinary function. The male turtle's tail, closely associated with reproductive activity, is long and relatively broad. The testes are carried within the body.

The female's tail is small by comparison, with the cloacal opening close to the base. Female turtles have two ovaries, each connected to the cloaca by an oviduct tube.

In some turtle species, there is virtually no courtship. In others, such as the painted turtles and the red-ears, the male has long claws on his front feet, and courts the female by swimming backward in front of her, vibrating his claws against her cheeks.

Mating occurs in the spring and may continue into summer. The male mounts the female and curls his long tail down and under her to achieve the union.

Wood turtles mating under water.

About two months after mating, the female selects a nest site, usually in loose, well-drained soil or sand. Here she digs a hole with her hind feet, deposits her eggs, and covers them over. The whole nesting operation may take from one to five hours, but once it is completed the female gives no further care to her young. Some turtles don't even bother to dig a nest.

The eggs incubate in the sunwarmed earth, and the baby turtles hatch in 60 to 90 days, fully equipped and completely on their own. If they should hatch too late in the fall, they simply hibernate in the nest until the following spring, when they emerge blinking and hungry.

DISTINGUISHING THE SEXES

We've already seen that male turtles have bigger tails than the females, and that in some water turtles the males have elongated claws on their front feet. In addition, the males of many species have concave plastrons, presumably as an aid in mounting the convex carapace of the female. These sex characteristics are not evident in young turtles.

This mature male sawback turtle illustrates the typically heavy tail of male turtles. A female's tail would be more slender.

Just out of the egg, this little diamondback takes one of his first cautious peeks at the strange world around him.

Adventuresome even at such a tender age, the young diamondback leaves his egg and ventures out to explore his new horizons.

LONGEVITY

The first question that may pop into a person's head whenever he sees a turtle is: I wonder how old he is? It's a fair enough question, because turtles *can* live a very long time. The life expectancy of a box turtle, for instance, is about a hundred years, and the giant Galapagos tortoise can make it to 150, or maybe more. Snapping turtles may live more than 50 years. The Philadelphia Zoo has had a common snapper for over 30 years, and it was no youngster when the Zoo got it.

So the turtle's reputation for longevity is based on some pretty good facts. However, a full-grown turtle is not *necessarily* old. Turtles do their fastest growing during the first five or six years of their lives, and most of them are mature by their seventh year. They continue growing after that, of course, but much more slowly.

SIZE

The largest turtle in the world is the leatherback. The carapace of a specimen from the Atlantic Ocean was eight feet in length; a specimen from the Pacific Ocean weighed 1900 pounds. These are maximum sizes; it is actually rare to find a leatherback more than 800 pounds.

The largest fresh water turtle by far is the alligator snapper, which often grows to 100 pounds, and *can* weigh as much as 200 pounds. The largest land turtle is the Galapagos tortoise, at 500 pounds.

These young painted turtles are scrambling to get out of their enclosure. The coin gives a good idea of the turtles' size.

On your mark, get set, go . . . notoriously slow, although many, particularly the water turtles, are streamlined, turtles take things slow and easy, which may in part account for their comparatively long lives.

These are three-striped mud turtles, one of the smallest turtles in the world. A full-grown male is just over 3 inches long.

The feet of water turtles are webbed to aid in propulsion through the water.

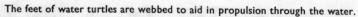

The turtle's shell provides protection for head and extremities. The less the need for protection, the less protective the shell.

You can always get a brisk argument going among the experts by stating which turtle is the smallest. Well, I like a good fight, so I'll stick my neck out and say the smallest turtle, in the U.S. at least, is the striped mud turtle of Florida. A full-grown male of this species is just over three inches long.

Turtles, by the way, are measured from the front edge of the carapace to the back edge, along an imaginary straight line (not across the curve of the shell). All sizes of individual turtles discussed in this book are given on this basis.

CLASSIFICATION

A "common" box turtle becomes pretty uncommon when you look at its scientific name: *Terrapene carolina carolina.* Scientific names, usually in Latin or Greek to resolve language differences, avoid the confusion created by the numerous local nicknames of an animal. Sometimes, however, the experts don't agree on the classification of certain turtles, and sometimes the turtles themselves lend confusion by hybridizing where their ranges overlap.

All turtles belong to the order Testudinata of the class Reptilia, but there are a number of separate families and genera.

TURTLE, TORTOISE, TERRAPIN

In the United States, the word *turtle* applies to fresh water turtles, to box and wood turtles, and to the big sea turtles. *Tortoise* refers to such strictly

Young snapping turtles like this one can be interesting pets, but older snapping turtles are dangerous.

land-going species as the desert, Berlandier's, and gopher tortoises. And the only *terrapins* are the diamondback terrapins of our coastal marshes and bays.

If you don't want to remember these distinctions, however, you can call them all "turtles" and be absolutely right.

TEMPERAMENT

If you pester a snapping turtle, he'll snap at you. So will a softshell turtle. And if either of them manages to latch on, you'll wish you'd stayed home.

Mud and musk turtles are often peevish when you first get them, but they become reasonably tame as soon as they find out you're not going to hurt them.

A few other turtles may make a show of opening their mouths when you pick them up, and if you actually stick your finger in, they will oblige by clamping down on it.

But with these few exceptions, turtles are among the most peaceable creatures on earth. A lot of them flatly refuse to bite, no matter what, which is one of the reasons why they make good pets.

2. Turtles as Pets

Take an elf, put him in a tortoise-shell house and endow him with patience, and you have a turtle—a whimsical little fellow who's fun to have around.

He won't respond to you with the bounding enthusiasm of a dog or the purring closeness of a cat, because the turtle is attuned to a world that's far removed from the world of dogs and cats and people.

No, your turtle won't respond in the manner of domesticated animals, but if you create a private world for him in an aquarium or terrarium, and make it as much like his natural home as possible, he'll soon adapt to it and right before your eyes will go about the ancient business of being a turtle.

He'll also learn that you are responsible for his food and will come waddling or paddling over whenever you approach his home. He'll probably never really enjoy being picked up and petted, but he'll be quiet, interesting, and attractive. And, after all, that's quite a bit, isn't it?

There are many varieties of turtles available today, including foreign species that dealers are beginning to import for the larger pet shops, and some of them make better pets than others. That is, some of them tame easily, eat heartily, stay within reasonable size limits, and live a long time—and others don't.

A baby musk turtle nestles comfortably in the hand.

I can tell you *in general* what to expect, but I hasten to add that just about the time you arrive at an all-embracing conclusion about a given turtle, along will come one non-conforming character who will knock your conclusion into a cocked hat.

With this in mind, let's take a look at the species you are most likely to encounter in the pet shops.

POPULAR WATER TURTLES

These turtles are excellent swimmers and spend most of their time in water, but they like to climb out on a sloping rock, log, or bank occasionally to rest and bask in the sun.

RED-EARED TURTLE (*Pseudemys scripta elegans*)—The red-ear is *the* turtle of the pet trade, the little green fellow with the red stripe behind each eye, seen in almost every pet shop. Red-ears hatch by the millions in the lower Mississippi Valley, particularly in Louisiana, and are about the size of a fifty-cent piece when they reach the stores. Most of them soon die because people either don't know how to take care of them or don't care to take the trouble. This is a shame, because turtles are not novelties, but living creatures that deserve a break.

Red-eared turtle, **Pseudemys scripta elegans,** the baby turtle most commonly offered for sale in pet shops.

Mobile turtle, peaceable and hardy, similar in appearance to the red-ear, but without the red stripe on the side of the head.

Red-ears are hardy; given reasonable care, they will thrive and grow, and be nice, attractive pets. Sometimes they're a little nervous when you first get them, but they calm down after they're with you awhile, and become quite tame. Fully grown, red-ears are 6 to 8 inches long. (Sizes given in this chapter are for turtles raised in captivity. In their natural habitat they usually grow larger.)

MOBILE TURTLE (*Pseudemys floridana mobiliensis*)—This is the second most common turtle in the pet trade. You'll find Mobiles mixed in with red-ears in the pet shops, and they're similar in appearance, but the Mobile doesn't have the red eye-stripes. Its markings are light yellow.

Mobiles are usually calm right from the start, and are among the tamest of the water turtles. They're hardy too, and eat very well, both meat and leafy vegetables. But there's one hitch: size. Mobiles are big turtles, the adults having shells 10 inches long or more, and the average home aquarium just isn't big enough to handle them. It takes a 50-gallon tank, at least, to properly accommodate a full-grown Mobile.

The common name of Mobile turtle is used here to designate all closely related sub-species and varieties of *Pseudemys floridana*. Some will consider that the name is perhaps used too all-embracingly, but it is useful in handling these comparatively large, peaceful turtles as a group.

Mississippi sawback turtle. Note the crescent behind the eye and the ridges on the back.

Baby southern painted turtle.

An adult eastern painted turtle.

MISSISSIPPI SAWBACK TURTLE (*Graptemys pseudogeographica kohnii*)
—Number three in the pet trade, the sawback or false map turtle is easy to
identify by its overall brown color, the vivid yellow or orange crescent behind
each eye, and the sharp ridges along its back. Male sawbacks grow to about
4 or 5 inches long, and females 6 to 7 inches long.

Mississippi sawbacks are not very easy to raise, and they're quite timid even
when full-grown. I've never seen a really tame sawback, but they're very
attractive turtles, especially when young. There are several related sub-species
(ringed sawback, midland sawback, and so on), and they're all interesting,
despite their timidity.

SOUTHERN PAINTED TURTLE (*Chrysemys picta dorsalis*)—In the pet
shops, along with the red-ears, Mobiles, and sawbacks, you'll occasionally see
a tiny dark brown turtle with a red stripe down the middle of its back and a
reddish-orange plastron with little or no plastral markings.

This is the southern painted turtle, which, like the red-ear, also hails from
the lower Mississippi Valley. Because of its small size (3 to 5 inches when
fully grown), its active, inquisitive nature, and its attractive appearance, it is
ideal for the home aquarium.

This is another turtle, however, that seldom becomes really tame. Approach
the turtle tank at any time, and your southern painted turtle will be off the
basking rock in a flash, heading for the safety of the bottom. Your friends who
think turtles are slow should see this little fellow in action!

Related painted turtles, less popular than *C.p. dorsalis*, are discussed under "Painted Turtles" on page 24.

And there you have the turtles that make up the bulk of the pet trade in the United States. Something like 14 million of these turtles are sold annually, and that's only part of the story. In the winter months, when turtle hatching in the southland stops, all but the largest existing stocks are sold out by mid-January. The demand for pet turtles keeps right on, however, so dealers are beginning to fill in the lean months with turtles flown in from southern Europe, South America, and Japan. There are three imported water turtles that you'll see fairly often nowadays, at least in the larger cities:

REEVES'S TURTLE (*Chinemys reevesi*)—This attractive little fellow from Japan and eastern China has a dark brown carapace, with three low parallel ridges running from front to back. The plastron is black, with pearly seams, and the chubby body is gray. There are faint white markings on the head and neck. Reeves's turtle is healthy, active, and friendly. When approached in the aquarium, this turtle will come paddling over as fast as he can; if a hand is put into the water, he'll climb right up on it and nose around for food. The mature size of this turtle is about 5 or 6 inches.

This fat and friendly visitor from the Orient is Reeves's turtle, now appearing regularly in American pet shops.

Three **Chinemys reevesi** at age about one month (above) and one of the same turtles at age of six months (below), showing rapid early growth typical of most turtles.

This is a Moorish pond turtle, a peppy little fellow from the Mediterranean region.

The yellow-spotted Amazon turtle, also called the sideneck turtle. Turtles just like this one have been living in the Amazon River and its tributaries for millions of years.

Podocnemis unifilis, the Amazon yellow-spotted turtle, seldom draws its head in when being handled. This turtle is more vegetarian than the most common North American baby aquatic turtles.

MOORISH POND TURTLE (*Clemmys leprosa*)—A spritely little fellow from southeastern Europe, the Moorish pond turtle has a grayish body and medium brown, low-keeled carapace. There are numerous light stripes on the head and neck, and a pale yellow dot behind each eye. Moorish pond turtles are active and nervous; although they may slow down a little as they get older, they can never be considered sluggish. Adult size, about 5 inches.

YELLOW-SPOTTED AMAZON TURTLE (*Podocnemis unifilis*)—This turtle, perhaps the most ancient of all living turtles, has been paddling around in tropical streams, exactly as we see him today, for many millions of years. His rounded carapace is olive-colored, and his plastron and body are pearly gray. His face is shaped something like a small bear's, and has bold yellow spots on it. When startled, he pulls his head in to the side, rather than straight in, as most other turtles do.

The books say that this turtle grows quite large, perhaps to 24 inches, but I have one that is nearly three years old at this writing, and still under 4 inches. Since turtles do their fastest growing in their first few years, I'd guess that the one I have won't go over 8 inches when fully grown. As to disposition, these turtles are methodical, calm, and peaceable. They even eat slowly, and with great dignity. But if you reach for them they'll move away fast enough.

WATER TURTLES OCCASIONALLY AVAILABLE

Besides the popular turtle species already discussed, you might also be able to acquire other water turtles. The turtles listed here are not generally available for sale on a regular basis, but an occasional specimen finds its way into the hands of a turtle keeper, either through purchase or capture.

PAINTED TURTLES (*Chrysemys picta picta, Chrysemys picta bellii, Chrysemys picta marginata*)—These small (maximum 6 inches), very attractive turtles abound in still waters almost everywhere in the United States. They have smooth, dark brown carapaces and clean yellow plastrons. The head has yellow markings, and the legs and back are striped with red.

Besides the popular southern painted turtle, previously discussed, there are three varieties of painted turtles, distinguished as follows: eastern paint, *C.p. picta*, red pattern around border of carapace, little or no pattern on plastron; western paint, *C.p. bellii*, little or no pattern around carapace, extensive dark pattern on plastron; midland paint, *C.p. marginata*, red carapace pattern similar to eastern variety, some markings on plastron.

These painted turtles are jumpy as grasshoppers when young, but usually become reasonably placid when they mature. However, their survival in the wild often depends on their ability to slide swiftly off the basking rock or log and head for safety in the mud and vegetation of the bottom, and this instinct stays with them throughout life, even in captivity. But the paints in general are a hardy clan, adjusting well to life in a large aquarium. With good care they will be quite active, and live a long time.

Baby eastern painted turtle. These turtles are common in ponds and streams of the eastern United States.

This is the yellow-bellied turtle, a pond-dweller from the southeastern United States, and a good pet.

YELLOW-BELLIED TURTLE (*Pseudemys scripta scripta*)—This is a nice docile turtle from the southeastern United States, easily recognized by the large yellow patch behind each eye and the bold black smudges forming a pattern around the underside of the carapace. The relatively short and deep shell is brownish, with a subdued pattern of light bars. Males grow to about $5\frac{1}{2}$ inches, females to $7\frac{1}{2}$ inches. These turtles usually make good pets; they are hardy, peaceable, and easy to tame.

COMMON MUSK TURTLE (*Sternotherus odoratus*)—The drab brown musk turtle, with its beady little eyes set in a mouselike face, seems an unlovely creature, and it is, particularly when you consider that it gives off a heavy musky odor and does not hesitate to snap out at the hand that attempts to grasp it. The only adornment of the musk turtle are two light lines running along each side of the head from the pointy nose back to the long neck.

But once a musk turtle gets used to captivity it will stop stinking and biting, and becomes not so unpleasant after all, but rather droll. It can even become a likable pet.

Given decent treatment, a musk turtle will reward its owner by becoming tame enough to take food from the fingers, by not taking up too much room (its size is under 5 inches), and by living a long, long time.

The common musk has three close relatives: Mississippi musk, loggerhead musk, and Tennessee musk. They all behave alike.

The musk turtle is a real ugly duckling, but his interesting antics will fascinate any turtle-keeper.

The skimpy plastron and long tail are characteristic of snapping turtles.

COMMON MUD TURTLE (*Kinosternon subrubrum subrubrum*)—Here is another ugly duckling, found in most of the eastern United States. It resembles the musk turtle, but its plastron is broader, and it lacks the musk's distinctive light lines on the head.

The mud turtle's disposition is always snappish when you first meet, but he calms down when he learns you're not going to hurt him, and he won't try to bite unless you tease him. He's under 5 inches long, hardy, and has been known to live 30 years in captivity. Both musk and mud turtles are "bottom crawlers," and neither are really good swimmers, so fix up a dry basking place *that's easy to climb out onto.*

Related varieties and species: Florida mud, Mississippi mud, Paradise Key mud, Sonoran mud, striped mud, yellow mud.

COMMON SNAPPING TURTLE (*Chelydra serpentina serpentina*)—Adult snappers are about 14 inches long and weigh 30 pounds or more, which is a bit large for the home aquarium. Also, they bite enthusiastically, which is a bit hard on the turtle owner. And finally, snappers are not the handsomest creatures on earth, except perhaps to other snappers. The dark brown carapace has three knobby keels, the plastron is skimpy, and the long, saw-toothed tail resembles that of an alligator. Common snappers are found in fresh water throughout the eastern and central United States, and are often used as food.

Despite all the disparaging remarks above, *young* snappers are not bad pets. They're interesting, very hardy, and willing to eat any kind of food you give them. *But don't keep them with turtles smaller than themselves!* It could be very rough on the smaller turtles. In fact it might be well to think the prospective purchase over carefully before you get a snapper at all. Your little snapper will get to be a big snapper, and then what will you do with it?

The common snapper, which also occurs in a slightly different form known as the Florida snapper, has only one close relative, the big alligator snapper.

SOUTHERN SOFT-SHELLED TURTLE (*Amyda ferox ferox*)—There's no mistaking this fellow! Its shell, as flat as the proverbial pancake, has an upper layer of leathery skin in place of the hornlike scutes. The soft-shelled turtle has an exceedingly long neck and a snout that looks like a schnorkel, which is just how he uses it.

Young softies are very lively, alert, and inquisitive. They make interesting pets, and they will quickly learn to take food from your fingers. They require an aquarium with a sandy bottom to bury themselves in and a smooth landing place out of water to rest on. This can be an old piece of smooth wood, or plastic—anything that won't injure their tender plastrons. Other turtles try to nibble on softies sometimes, so *keep your softies in a separate tank.*

Here again, the warning on snappers holds true. Softies, too, grow up to become big, tough, and very dangerous. Think this over carefully before you take on one of the little ones.

Soft-shelled turtles are interesting when young, but they are dangerous when mature. Soft-shells like to dig into the aquarium gravel.

Baby eastern diamondback terrapin. Diamondbacks are always actively curious, and usually tame, but they are too big for the average home turtle tank when fully grown.

Adult eastern diamondback terrapin.

The southern soft-shelled turtle is from Florida, and he has six close relatives: Agassiz', eastern spiny, Emory's, southern spiny, spineless, and western spiny.

NORTHERN DIAMONDBACK TERRAPIN (*Malaclemys terrapin terrapin*)—Here's a real extrovert, a rollicking pirate from the salt marshes of the eastern United States.

Terrapins do fairly well in captivity in fresh water, if you give them plenty of room. They eat heartily, are afraid of nothing, and can live several years with good care (but live much longer in nature). Unfortunately for the turtle hobbyist, diamondbacks get quite large: females about $7\frac{1}{2}$ inches, males something like $5\frac{1}{2}$ inches, both with heavy, chunky bodies. And because they're so vigorous, they can keep a tank in a constant state of upheaval.

Related varieties are the southern, mangrove, Florida, Mississippi, and Texas diamondbacks.

SPOTTED TURTLES AND BOG TURTLES

I've tucked the spotted and bog turtles in between the water turtles and the land turtles because, in my opinion, that's where they are in nature. Their back feet do not have the well-defined paddles of the water turtles, but are

29

Note the striking resemblance between this spotted turtle (right) and wood turtle. Both turtles are within the same genus.

The scattered spots to which this spotted turtle owes its popular name form a pleasing pattern.

shaped like those of the wood turtle, to which they're related under the genus *Clemmys* (along with the Pacific pond turtle). Feet shaped like this indicate a creature that can navigate either on land or in water, and while the spotted and bog turtles do spend about 95 percent of their time in shallow water, they are not so completely aquatic as the true water turtles. Obviously, their home in captivity should have a large land area as well as a water area.

SPOTTED TURTLE (*Clemmys guttata*)—This little turtle's head and shell are black with yellow spots. The throat has yellow stripes, the legs are dark on top and yellow underneath, and the plastron is yellow and black.

Spotted turtles live in shallow ponds and bogs, but occasionally will move about on land, rarely straying far from the water. They used to abound in the northern and eastern United States, but they're becoming rare in some areas and have disappeared entirely from others.

These turtles rarely exceed $4\frac{1}{2}$ inches, so there's no problem in housing them, and they are quite gentle. However, they're often very sensitive to their environment. Some collectors have good luck with them, and others have no luck at all.

MUHLENBERG'S (BOG) TURTLE (*Clemmys muhlenbergii*)—Muhlenberg's turtle inhabits northern and eastern sphagnum bogs and marshy lowlands in small and widely scattered colonies. Unfortunately, there are no longer many of these turtles to be found.

An orange blotch on the head is a characteristic of Muhlenberg's bog turtle, a pleasing turtle that is becoming rare over most of its range.

Clemmys muhlenbergii is a small turtle, under 4 inches long, with a vivid orange blotch on each side of the head, behind the eyes. The shell is moderately domed, has a slight keel, and is dark brown with more or less faint orange markings. The neck, legs, and tail are dark brown with reddish overtones.

I know of only a few *C. muhlenbergii* in captivity (one active male is in my collection), but these few are doing very well. They're healthy and eat heartily at every feeding. Some tend to be a little snappy, but they're not big enough to do more than pinch your finger smartly.

If you are fortunate enough to have one of these frisky little turtles, take good care of it, because it's one of a vanishing breed. In fact, I'd like to see a far-sighted zoo, aquarium, or private estate establish a breeding colony of Muhlenberg's bog turtles. They might just wind up with the only remaining colony on earth.

WOOD AND BOX TURTLES

These are basically land turtles, but both have some affinity for water, the wood turtle more so than the box turtle.

WOOD TURTLE (*Clemmys insculpta*)—This is probably the most intelligent, alert, and active turtle in or out of captivity. It's also a hardy turtle, and it does very well in captivity if given good care and a *roomy* enclosure with a pool in it.

The wood turtle is a very attractive fellow with a low, deeply sculptured brown carapace. The plastron is yellow, with a large dark smudge on the outer portion of each plate. The head, legs, and tail are brown, blending into brick red or orange near the body. Adult male turtles are about 7½ inches long; females 6½ inches.

Wood turtles are capable swimmers and spend quite a bit of time in the water. They hibernate in mud on the bottom of streams and ponds in the winter, mate in water in the spring, and in hot weather return to water to cool off. The rest of the time they range through all sorts of terrain, but they usually seem to return to a "home" area.

Wood turtles make excellent, long-lived pets, but their collection and possession is illegal in some parts of the United States.

BOX TURTLE (*Terrapene carolina*)—Rare indeed is the American boy who hasn't at some time come home from summer camp, vacation, or a hike in the woods without a box turtle in hand. And if *you* see a turtle strolling across a road, farm, or your own lawn—especially on a rainy day—chances are it's a box turtle. This is probably the most familiar turtle in the United States, the little fellow that can pull in his head and legs and close up like a box when startled.

The wood turtle, perhaps the most alert and intelligent of all turtles, is protected by many state conservation departments, as are some other turtles.

Eastern box turtle, one month old.

Eastern box turtle, one year old.

The carapace is highly domed, and the coloring usually consists of yellow or orange markings on a dark brown background, or vice versa, arranged in many striking patterns. The shell length is usually under 6 inches.

Box turtles are not very aquatic. They swim awkwardly, if at all, and enter shallow water only to drink or to go a-wading. They're usually found, however, in low, damp places *near* water, except on rainy days, when they wander all over the landscape.

There are two species of box turtles in the United States: the ornate box turtle and the eastern box turtle. The eastern box turtle occurs in four varieties: common box, Florida box, Gulf Coast box and three-toed box—plus a large number of intergrade specimens wherever two or more ranges overlap.

Box turtles make good long-lived pets, if given the same reasonable care you'd give any valued pet. To illustrate, let me tell you about a male box turtle, an old trooper named "Mike."

Back when vaudeville was in its heyday, a young married couple had a dancing-juggling act. They traveled the Keith and Orpheum circuits from 1918 to about 1935, billed as "*Lorette and Morton.*"

And wherever they went, a young and frisky turtle named Mike went with them, sharing their hotel rooms and dressing rooms all over the country.

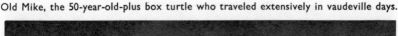

Old Mike, the 50-year-old-plus box turtle who traveled extensively in vaudeville days.

Eastern box turtle, two years old.

Eastern box turtle, six years old.

Today the golden era is over, and the distaff member of the act, who in private life is Mrs. Christine Layre, lives quietly in her modest home in Philadelphia. A few years ago her husband passed away, but Mrs. Layre is not alone. Mike, the old turtle trooper, is with her, and still going strong.

Not long ago Mrs. Layre brought Mike to visit our turtles. We put him in the "Turtlearium" where, as a testimonial to his vigor, he promptly began courting all the lady box turtles.

"You know," said Mrs. Layre as she sipped her coffee, "old Mike has the run of the house, and he's as playful as a kitten. When I'm watching TV, he comes in and nips at my shoes, and unties the laces, and just keeps *pestering* until I pay some attention to him.

"And what an appetite! He eats chopped raw beef, canned fish, medium boiled eggs, all kinds of cheese—especially Swiss—strawberries, tomatoes, cantaloupe, peaches, grapes, and lettuce.

"I don't know how old Mike is, but he's been with me since 1917. Friends of ours found him in the woods near Woodhaven, Long Island, and gave him to us. He was full-grown even then, so I guess he must be well over fifty."

Mrs. Layre sipped her coffee and looked back through the years. "My husband loved Mike," she said. "I retired from show business early, but he kept right on, and whenever he came in off the road the first thing he'd say was, 'Where's Mike?'."

"And I'd kid him and say, 'I don't know, maybe he got out.' Well, the turtle hunt would be on! We'd look in corners and under chairs until we found him. Then we'd laugh and make a big fuss over him, and Mike would be happy."

Then Mrs. Layre smiled softly and added, "Of course that was years ago, when we and Mike were young."

TORTOISES

This is the amiable, unhurried character of the fable "The Tortoise and the Hare," and he's a real land-lubber. A look at his heavy shell, stubby legs, and completely un-flippered feet will show you that water is definitely *not* Mr. Tortoise's element. He drinks water, of course, and further meets his moisture requirements by eating succulent green vegetation. In hot weather he may sit awhile in water—very shallow water—to soak. And that's the total of the tortoise's relationship with water.

Tortoises are droll, gentle creatures and make interesting, even lovable, pets—but they are very hard to keep alive for any length of time in captivity. I know of very few tortoises that have lived for more than two years in captivity, including those in zoos (with the exception of the giant Galapagos tortoises, which can hardly be classified as house pets). In my opinion, you'll do well to skip the tortoises, and turn to other turtles for pets, unless you are prepared to go to a lot of trouble to maintain them properly. Of course if you live in Florida, and want a gopher tortoise, or in the Southwest, and want a

This handsome tortoise is Berlandier's tortoise, found in semi-arid areas, but less tolerant of true desert conditions than its cousin, the desert tortoise. Both turtles look alike, but the desert tortoise is usually lighter in color.

A sunny, dry, grassy area is the perfect home ground for many of the land turtles.

Hermann's tortoise is difficult to keep in captivity, but well worth the effort for anyone who is successful at providing for its needs.

Gopher tortoises like the one pictured here dig extensive burrows and sometimes share them with many other creatures, from foxes to rattlesnakes.

Berlandier's tortoise, go ahead. You'll have a good chance of keeping them alive in the climate they're used to.

There are three tortoises native to the United States: the Gopher tortoise (*Gopherus polyphemus*), which inhabits sandy, wooded areas from southwestern South Carolina through central Florida and the Gulf States; Berlandier's tortoise (*Gopherus berlandieri*), which is found in the same kind of terrain in southern Texas; and the desert tortoise (*Gopherus agassizi*), which lives in arid areas in southern Nevada, southeastern California, and southwestern Arizona.

All three of these toroises are large (over 10 inches long), with heavy shells, usually of some shade of brown or tan. They have elephant-like hind feet and shovel-shaped front feet. They have a penchant for digging extensive burrows, to which they retreat when the weather is either too chilly or too hot.

There is another tortoise that is turning up more and more frequently in our pet shops, and this is Hermann's tortoise (*Testudo hermanni*), which is imported from several countries bordering the Mediterranean. In size and shape, Hermann's tortoise is similar to the American tortoises described above, but the coloring is different. The shell of Hermann's tortoise is a greenish ivory, with black markings in each shield.

His disposition is typically tortoise—calm, peaceable, and unhurried. Unfortunately, Hermann's tortoise is, like the other tortoises, difficult to maintain as a pet, and does not live long in captivity. We do not know much about the real needs of these gentle creatures, and until we do we should leave them in their natural habitat. They too are entitled to life.

3. Your Turtle's Home

Your turtle will probably spend his whole life in the home you fix up for him, so make it as pleasant and comfortable as you can.

Water turtles need enough clean water to swim freely in, and a dry area that they can climb onto easily to rest and bask.

Land turtles such as box turtles, wood turtles, and tortoises need plenty of land to walk about on, and a shallow pool of water for wading and drinking.

AQUARIUMS FOR WATER TURTLES

A standard 5-gallon rectangular glass tank will accommodate three or four baby water turtles for about a year, or one turtle for about three years. I strongly advise against getting a smaller aquarium, because your turtle will grow, and you won't want him to wind up looking like a hippo in a brandy glass.

The water should be two to three inches deep, and about 75 degrees F. Whenever you change the water, make sure that the fresh water is roughly the same temperature as the old water.

The landing or basking place can be a sloping rock or small log, a plastic "island" suspended from the top, or any similar object that the turtles can climb onto *easily*. It should have an adequate dry area to allow the turtles to dry themselves completely, including their plastrons. The landing place

A large aquarium for water turtles is easily maintained, as the clarity of the water attests. The rocks arranged in platform fashion serve to provide both a basking space and shade.

This aquarium houses two softshell turtles, one of which has dug itself in under the filter. A filter in a turtle tank can be of great use in keeping the water clean, reducing the necessity for frequent water changes. The plastic shelving arrangement allows the turtles a place to bask.

The turtles in this aquarium are able to receive the benefits of some sunshine without being put into the open.

Always on the alert for enemies, baby turtles are ready to dash off their basking rocks and swim to safety at the first hint of danger.

should have enough texture to give traction for climbing, but no sharp edges that might injure the turtles' plastrons as they slide off.

Equip your aquarium with a reflector light containing a 40-watt bulb. This will provide both light and warmth. Basking and drying under a warm light seems to be an enjoyable pastime for turtles, and, in addition, may serve to retard or prevent fungal infections.

This meets the basic housing requirements for water turtles, but if you want to get classy—and save yourself a lot of cleaning—cover the bottom of the aquarium with coarse gravel, to a depth of about 1½ inches, and install a filter. There are inside filters, undergravel filters, and outside filters. They're all operated by air pumps, and all are effective, if the water is deep enough. The gravel will add to the natural appearance of your setup, and the filter will help keep it clean. Besides, your turtles will have fun playing in the air bubbles.

TERRARIUMS FOR LAND TURTLES

The indoor terrarium I have rigged up for my land turtles is a box, 6 feet long, 3 feet wide, and 1 foot high. The bottom, sides, and back are of ¾-inch plywood. The front is glass. This terrarium rests on six legs, made of 2 × 4's, 24 inches high.

Small round pebbles cover the bottom to a depth of about 2 inches. That's *round pebbles*, not crushed aggregate, which is too sharp. You can get round

One end of this terrarium has a light burning over it, and the other end is kept shaded. In this way the animals can vary their surroundings. The pebbles are rounded to eliminate damage to the turtles.

pebbles at any good building supply yard, for about $1.50 per hundred pounds.

A shallow earthenware "pool" with sloping sides is sunk into the pebbles to provide a wading area and drinking supply. And here a word of caution is necessary: *the pool can be a death trap if the sides are too high, or too steep, or too slick.* Turtles can fall in, and they invariably land upside down. A turtle in this fix arches his neck to flip over, which puts his head under water, and unless someone hauls him out he can drown.

One end of the terrarium is quite warm; the other end is cooler, and sort of woodsy. I arranged this by hanging a metal lamp, with a 50-watt bulb in it, over one end, and covering this end with a large sheet of glass. This keeps the temperature up around 80 degrees.

The "cool" end has no lamp, and no glass cover. This end of the terrarium contains the pool, plus some green plants in low pots sunk into the pebbles. The wood and box turtles spend most of their time at this end, the tortoises at the warmer end. From time to time, however, all the turtles wander all over the terrarium.

Sparsely furnished terrariums can be decorated from above simply yet tastefully with potted plants.

This is one of the author's many terrariums for housing land turtles and tortoises. The water receptacle is shallow, because a deep pan could be a death trap.

At home in the greenery.

The inside of the terrarium is painted green, and the outside is a lighter color, a sort of off-green. I used three coats, to protect the wood against moisture and keep it from warping. The terrarium is inexpensive, attractive, and functional. Most important of all, the turtles like it.

For summer use I have an area in my backyard, about 6 feet square, enclosed by a low stone wall. In this are some low shrubs for shade, some ground cover plants which the turtles like to poke around in, and the pool from the terrarium. I rinse the pool every day with the garden hose and fill it with fresh water.

4. Foods and Feeding

WATER TURTLES

I feed my water turtles lean raw beef, chopped up fine, and liberally fortified with liquid multivitamins and bone meal. I use a drop of vitamins and a pinch of bone meal per tablespoon of meat, mixed in well so it won't wash off in the water. About once a week I feed them chopped raw fish or shrimp, prepared the same way, for variety. Dried turtle foods can be fed for variety.

My turtles eat three times a week (Mondays, Wednesdays and Saturdays). I feed them in the laundry tub, in about three inches of 75-degree F. water. This helps keep their tanks clean, and it's a lot easier to rinse the tub than it would be to siphon out several large tanks after each feeding. I give them an hour or so to eat a full meal, then remove them from the tub and rinse it. As a precaution against plugging the drain, I put a strainer upside down over the outlet.

Finally, I keep a fresh leaf of lettuce in the tanks for the turtles to nibble on between meals. Some of them also like a sliver of cucumber or banana once in a while. (Feed spotted and bog turtles as you would water turtles, but offer them some of the things listed below as well.)

Many turtles and tortoises can be tamed to accept food from the fingers.

One way to avoid having to change the water too frequently is to feed aquatic turtles in a container separate from their regular living quarters. Leave the turtles in the feeding container for about two hours after feeding; elimination is swift, and in this way none of the food and little of the turtles' droppings will foul the water of their home tank.

WOOD AND BOX TURTLES

These turtles will thrive on a diet of bananas and chopped lean raw beef, both laced with vitamins and bone meal. For the most part they prefer the meat, but a turtle that has been a consistent meat eater will sometimes suddenly switch to bananas for awhile, and vice versa, so provide them with both, alternately. Box and wood turtles also like strawberries, grapes, melons, cucumbers, tomatoes, and so on. Remember that turtles like variety, just like people, and have individual tastes. Give them their basic diet of meat and bananas, but offer them other things as well.

TORTOISES

The standard diet for my tortoises consists of dog kibble, bananas, a little chopped beef, tomatoes, plenty of lettuce and other succulent greens, plus vitamins and bone meal, of course. I soak the dog chow in water, to which a few drops of vitamins have been added, until it's soft. My tortoises get the chow at one meal, bananas the next, with a little meat and lots of green at every meal. I give them the greens last, or they fill up on greens and ignore the rest of the food. I also give them tomatoes about once a week, and offer them all the foods listed above for box and wood turtles from time to time, plus

A favorite position for baby turtles: piled up one on top of another in a corner of the tank. The turtle needs quantities of bone-building nutrients for proper shell development.

pancakes, and *clover*. They dearly love clover in season. As with all turtles, it's a good idea to give tortoises a wide variety of foods.

VITAMINS AND BONE MEAL

I've mentioned vitamins and bone meal several times, for good reason. They're both very important. In their natural habitat, turtles get a lot of sunshine, plus other factors that they don't get in captivity. Liquid vitamins help make up for the deficiency. And bone meal provides calcium for bone and shell growth, which is extremely important. Both vitamins and bone meal should be mixed into all the food your turtles eat.

5. Temperature and Cleanliness

Most turtles can live comfortably at about 75 degrees F. If your house temperature stays at about 72 degrees F., the use of reflector lights on the aquarium and lamps on the terrarium will give enough additional heat to keep them cozy. Some turtle-keepers use white bulbs during the day and blue bulbs at night. The latter provide warmth and give the turtles a rest from the glare of the white bulbs.

Other turtle-keepers use thermostatically-controlled aquarium heaters. These are excellent, and not too expensive. Others (the aristocrats) equip their whole setup with automatic temperature and humidity controls.

This room is equipped with temperature and humidity control devices to allow year-round maintenance of both rare and common turtles.

The turtle's eyes should be clear. Regularly check your turtles for symptoms of illness.

Whatever method you use, proper temperature is very important. If your turtles get too warm, they'll die. Don't ever set them on a radiator! If they get too cold, they'll stop eating, and northern varieties may attempt to hibernate. *They cannot hibernate successfully indoors,* not even in a fairly cool basement. They may go to sleep, but as indoor temperatures never reach the continuous low of the outdoors, they'll continue to burn up energy and eventually starve. Keep your turtles at about 75 to 80 degrees F. and they'll do fine.

Proper humidity is very important too. See "Pneumonia" on page 53.

Turtles should be kept clean—for their health and your pleasure.

I change the water in the tanks once a week, at the same time changing the charcoal in the filters. And once a month I take everything out of the tanks and give the whole works a good scrubbing. This keeps fungi and algae from getting a foothold and keeps the tanks sparkling clean and sweet-smelling.

In the terrarium, I change the pool water every day, and once a month I wash the whole terrarium with soap and water. To do this, I push the pebbles aside and scrub the bottom of half of the terrarium. When this dries, I scrub the other half. Land turtles sometimes get mites, but usually not if they're kept clean. If yours do, however, a dusting of *Dri-Die 67*, which destroys the outer layer of the arthropod's body, will get rid of them. Do not use chemical insecticides, as they are poisonous to cold-blooded animals.

6. Turtle Diseases And Their Treatment

Turtles are generally hardy but, like people, they sometimes get sick. Their most common ailments are pneumonia, soft shell, swollen eyes, fungus, plastral sores, constipation, and loss of appetite, none of which is transferable to humans. You can get right in there and take care of your sick little friend with no fear of catching a bug.

And you *should* treat a pet turtle when it's sick, because if it's worth having at all, it's worth taking care of. We'll discuss what is known about these ailments in a moment, but first I want to describe how to give turtles medicine orally. This information applies throughout much of this chapter.

GIVING MEDICINE ORALLY

To give medicine orally to my larger turtles, I first pry the mouth open—*very carefully*—with the flat tapered end of an orangewood cuticle stick. The orangewood is tough, but it's not sharp, and it won't splinter. You could also use any similar object that will open the turtle's mouth without damaging it. Whatever you use, *be gentle*.

When the turtle's mouth is open, administer the medicine with a plastic dropper. If the medicine is in tablet form, crush it and dissolve it in a little

When picking up adult turtles, especially adult water turtles like this painted turtle, grasp the turtle so as to minimize danger from jaws and claws.

52

water in a teaspoon. If it's a capsule, break it open and dissolve the contents in a little water. It's dangerous to put pills, or dry powders, in turtles' mouths, as turtles choke very easily.

After the pill or capsule is dissolved, add a drop or two of multivitamins to the solution. Some medicines are a little rough on the turtle's nervous system, and the vitamins (particularly the B group) will help offset the effect. Besides, they help perk up the appetite, which is always desirable.

It's almost impossible to administer medicines orally to small turtles, or to stubborn turtles, without injuring them. In these cases, mix the medicine into their food, or dissolve it in their drinking water. Sometimes, in the case of water turtles, you can put it into the water in which they are fed, or you can hold a particularly stubborn turtle upside down and put the medicine around his mouth with the dropper. The turtle may open his mouth in protest—and in goes the medicine.

You have to play it by ear and administer the medicine the best way you can without injuring the patient. ONE IMPORTANT WORD OF CAUTION: *if your turtle is in a weakened condition, do not attempt to give it medicine by mouth at all.* Turtles choke easily at any time, and when they are weak the medicine is very likely to enter the lungs and drown them.

PNEUMONIA

Turtles are subject to a form of respiratory infection which, in its advanced stages, is the most serious disease a pet turtle can contract. Called pneumonia because of the resemblance of the disease to the human respiratory infection, the disease is treatable only if caught early. In the initial stages, the turtle may grow sluggish, stop eating, and open and close its mouth like a fish. Its nose may be runny, and it may wheeze when it breathes. If the disease gets worse, the turtle will display obvious difficulty in breathing, gasping strenuously for breath. At this point the disease is almost always fatal, and the only treatment I can suggest is prayer.

Luckily, pneumonia can be cured in its earlier stages. The trick is to detect the condition as soon as it starts, isolate the sick turtle to protect your other turtles, and begin treatment immediately.

You can treat infected turtles with either antibiotics or antihistamines, administered orally. Among the antibiotics, Aureomycin is good, and so is Acromycin. You might want to start with one, and if it doesn't seem to be taking effect in a day or two, switch to the other. They're both broad-spectrum antibiotics, and between the two you're pretty sure to hit all the respiratory bugs. Your veterinarian will give you a prescription.

As for dosage, an 8-inch turtle gets about 25 milligrams of the antibiotic once a day for three days. Larger turtles should get a little more, smaller turtles correspondingly less. That should do the trick. If it doesn't, skip two days without giving the medicine, then resume treatment for two more days.

That's all. Avoid overdosing, because antibiotics are basically toxic, and there's no point in killing your turtle with medicine while you're trying to cure him of pneumonia.

Many turtle-keepers prefer antihistamines for pneumonia, because they're fairly effective, especially in the earlier stages of the disease, and because they have the advantage of not being toxic if used sensibly. Both Coricidin and Super Anahist are good brands. The dosage is 1/8th to 1/4th tablet—depending on the size of the turtle—crushed and dissolved in a little water (with a drop or two of vitamins), and administered orally twice a day for two days. This dosage allows for spillage, so the turtle is actually getting only about 1/16th to 1/8th of a tablet, which is plenty.

No one knows for certain what causes respiratory infections in turtles, but apparently big fluctuations in temperature and, particularly, in humidity, have a lot to do with it. A fairly high humidity seems to be important for all turtles, with the exception of desert tortoises. Pneumonia is most prevalent in the winter, when the windows are shut and the house heated. Things get pretty dry then, and unless you take steps to boost the humidity your turtles will suffer. Glass covers over the aquariums and terrariums, with half an inch or so left open for air, will help maintain the humidity inside the enclosures. A pan of water on the radiator (if any) in the turtle room will help, too. And it's a good idea to sprinkle the pebbles in the terrarium daily. Of course, the very best thing is an automatically controlled humidifier, if you can afford one.

There's also a possibility that turtles contract respiratory infections from people. This is conjecture, but just to make sure I always wash my hands with soap and water before handling my turtles or mixing their food. And when I have a cold, I stay away from them as much as possible.

SOFT SHELL

Soft shell is the result of a dietary deficiency, a lack of sufficient calcium. To correct the condition, add more bone meal to the food. When the shell is very soft, immediate help is required, so mix hefty doses of powdered calcium into both the food and the water. You can get calcium at your druggist's, and don't stint. It's cheap. If the turtle is not eating, you can dissolve calcium in water, add a drop or two of vitamins, and administer it orally. Or you can load the turtle's drinking or swimming water with calcium, add a little vitamins, and leave it in a couple of days. Then, when its appetite picks up, load the food with calcium until the shell is hard again.

It's best, of course, to *prevent* soft shell, and you can do this by making sure your turtles get enough calcium by mixing plenty of bone meal (and powdered calcium if you want to be doubly sure) in all their food, including lettuce, fruits, and vegetables. You can also get little calcium blocks (they're sometimes shaped like turtles) at your pet shop, and drop one in each tank and pool. Replace them every month or so, when they will have dissolved.

LOSS OF APPETITE

Some turtles eat heartily at every meal; others are hearty eaters part of the time, skimpy eaters the rest of the time; a few are chronic non-eaters. All turtles have a tendency to stop eating when the temperature drops, so try to keep it up around 75 degrees F. at all times.

If you have a hearty eater, congratulations. If you have an on-again-off-again eater, you can help him over the lean periods by giving him liquid multivitamins orally, or in his drinking water, and tempting him with different kinds of foods. Try him on earthworms or the meal worms that pet shops sell. Many water turtles will greedily gobble *Tubifex* worms, also sold in pet shops, but these worms live in filth and harbor disease. Fresh strawberries are good, too (for land turtles), and in the winter you can get frozen ones (without syrup).

If you have a fairly good eater that suddenly goes off its feed, raise the temperature in the enclosure to about 80 degrees F. (but not over that) for a day or two, and tempt him with different kinds of foods as mentioned above. If the hunger strike continues for more than a week, give him liquid multivitamins orally. About 0.6 cc. a day for three or four days should start him eating. If you can't get his mouth open easily, put the vitamins in his drinking or swimming water.

Once in a while there will be a turtle that will flatly refuse to eat in captivity. If you should get one of these chronic non-eaters, the best thing you can do is release him in a suitable place, well away from roads, where there are others of his kind. Release him in the summer or early fall, so he'll have plenty of time to adjust before cold weather sets in. Never release a turtle in the late fall. If your non-eater is not a local variety, then the best thing you can do is to try to coax him to eat with warmth and vitamins. With patience, this often works.

FUNGUS

Fungus is indicated by white or gray spots on the turtle's body or, sometimes, on the shell. It very often starts with the feet, then spreads.

You can clear up fungus by applying commerical aquarium fungicides to the infected areas once a day for several days, or by putting a teaspoonful of the solution per gallon of water in the turtle tank. It's also a good idea to put a little in the tanks once a month to *prevent* fungus. Pet stores sell these products for the treatment of fungus in tropical fish and turtles.

SWOLLEN EYES

Swollen eyes are the result of poor diet, poor living conditions, a bacterial infection—or all three. To prevent this ailment, follow the suggestions on turtle care given in the previous chapter. To cure it, treat the eyes daily with a paste made of Aureomycin and water, or penicillin ointment, until they are

Turtles vary in their capacities to stretch their necks. Some are able to extend the head a remarkable distance, and in others the head can be extended to only a short distance greater than normal.

open and clear. Then take better care of your turtle so his eyes won't go shut again.

PLASTRAL SORES

Plastral sores, or pitted areas on the plastron that will become sores, are caused in water turtles by a too-rough basking rock. In land turtles they're caused by constant contact with an abrasive surface such as rough cement, or because the turtle sits too long in his own excrement.

Change your water turtles' basking rock to a smoother one, or use a small log or a suspended plastic island. Encourage your land turtles to move around more by providing roomier, more natural quarters with a wading pool.

Treat plastral sores by washing the plastron daily and applying turtle fungicide full strength until the affected areas are healed. Or you can paint the plastron with zephiran chloride or a dilute solution of potassium permanganate. I've never used either of the latter, but other turtle-keepers say they are okay.

CONSTIPATION

Tortoises are the fellows most likely to be troubled by constipation, and it can be very serious if not relieved. The best treatment is a simple one: let the tortoise soak for about half an hour in lukewarm shallow water. It's also a good idea to give new tortoises this treatment, because they're very often bound up when you first get them. You may want to give your tortoises this treatment about twice a month thereafter, just on general principle. Even if they don't need it, they'll enjoy it.

WORMS

Roundworms are slender white worms. If you see any of them in the tank, you're stuck with an infestation. I've never had this problem with my turtles, but a noted zoo veterinarian suggests that one of the piperazine compounds, administered orally in a proportion of 100 mg. for each pound of turtle, will kill the worms. You might want to check this with your own vet, or with your druggist.

And of course common sense tells us to give the infested tank a good scrubbing, followed by a minute examination, to make sure the worms are all gone.

CUTS AND BITES

Isolate the injured turtle so the other turtles can't nip at him. Then clean the injured area and apply either merthiolate or penicillin ointment (never use mercurochrome; it's poison to turtles). The little cotton swabs, such as Q-Tips, packaged by the pharmaceutical houses, are very handy for applying medications externally.

"TLC"

"TLC" is a hospital term that is sometimes used jokingly, but shouldn't be. It means "Tender Loving Care."

The curved horny jaws of this land turtle are useful to it in tearing and crushing its food.

It means that patients are properly treated not with medicine alone, but with sympathy and understanding as well.

On a larger scale, Tender Loving Care can mean our rightful attitude toward *all* living things, especially those delivered into our hands for safekeeping, whose very lives depend on us.

It means that we give these dependent creatures the best care we can, including nourishing food, fresh water, and a decent home.

It means that we are sensitive to their needs, so that if they are sick or hurt, we know it immediately, and give them prompt attention.

It means that we give them our *presence* once in a while, so they'll know they're not forsaken. Oh yes, they'll know.

Dr. Albert Schweitzer summed it up beautifully in his prayer for animals, which ends like this:

"*. . . and for those who deal with them we ask a heart of compassion and gentle hands and kindly words. Make us, ourselves, to be true friends to animals and so to share the blessing of the merciful.*"

7. Pictorial Gallery of Exotic Turtles

Missy, the "mystery" turtle. Although she is some form of box turtle, no one has yet been able to identify her definitely. Her carapace and plastron are of a uniform horn color, with no trace of a pattern. Her head, tail, legs, and body are dark brown, also with no pattern. Can you identify her?

This is a mature dwarf diamondback terrapin, a true dwarf, not a baby.

Chersine angulata, from Africa.

Mud turtle, from Trinidad.

South American red-footed tortoise.

The large South American red-footed tortoise glares at little Hermann's tortoise impertinently crossing his path.

Malayemys subtrijuga, from Malaya.

In Japan, this turtle goes by the common name Madori kame.

Homopus aureolatus, from Africa.

Red-headed turtle, from Trinidad.

BIBLIOGRAPHY

HANDBOOK OF TURTLES
 by Archie Carr.
A good, thoroughgoing, scientific reference to North American turtles. 542 pages. Published (1952) by Cornell University Press, Ithaca, N. Y. Price $8.50.

A FIELD GUIDE TO REPTILES AND AMPHIBIANS
 by Roger Conant, Curator of Reptiles, Philadelphia Zoological Society.
Excellent for identification of turtles of the eastern United States and Canada, including baby turtles. The color plates are particularly useful for this purpose. Published (1958) by Houghton Mifflin Company, Boston. 366 pages. Price about $4.50.

TURTLES OF THE UNITED STATES AND CANADA
 by Clifford Pope.
The scientific names of some of the turtles have been changed since this book was published, but it's still a very good work on turtle habits. Published (1939) by Alfred A. Knopf, New York. 343 pages. Price $4.50.